101 FACTS ABOUT

DESERTS

Julia Barnes

Gareth Stevens Publishing
A WORLD ALMANAC EDUCATION GROUP COMPANY

Please visit our web site at: www.garethstevens.com
For a free color catalog describing Gareth Stevens Publishing's
list of high-quality books and multimedia programs,
call 1-800-542-2595 (USA) or 1-800-387-3178 (Canada).
Gareth Stevens Publishing's fax: (414) 332-3567.

Library of Congress Cataloging-in-Publication Data

Barnes, Julia, 1955-
    101 facts about deserts / by Julia Barnes. — North American ed.
      p. cm. — (101 facts about our world)
    Summary: Describes the characteristics, formation, plant and animal life,
and preservation of deserts.
    Includes bibliographical references and index.
    ISBN 0-8368-3706-1 (lib. bdg.)
    1. Desert ecology—Juvenile literature. 2. Deserts—Juvenile literature. [1. Deserts.
2. Desert ecology. 3. Ecology.] I. Title: One hundred one facts about deserts.
II. Title: One hundred and one facts about deserts. III. Title: Deserts. IV. Title.
QH541.5.D4B37   2003
551.41'5—dc21   2003045713

This North American edition first published in 2004 by
Gareth Stevens Publishing
A World Almanac Education Group Company
330 West Olive Street, Suite 100
Milwaukee, WI 53212 USA

This U.S. edition copyright © 2004 by Gareth Stevens, Inc. Original edition © 2003 by First
Stone Publishing. First published by First Stone Publishing, 4/5 The Marina, Harbour
Road, Lydney, Gloucestershire, GL15 5ET, United Kingdom. Additional end matter © 2004
by Gareth Stevens, Inc.

First Stone Series Editor: Claire Horton-Bussey
First Stone Designer: Rob Benson
Geographical consultant: Miles Ellison
Gareth Stevens Editors: Catherine Gardner and JoAnn Early Macken

Photographs © Oxford Scientific Films Ltd

Printed in Hong Kong through Printworks Int. Ltd

1 2 3 4 5 6 7 8 9 07 06 05 04 03

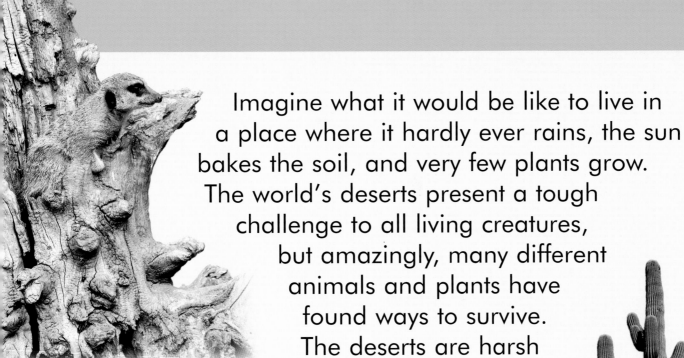

Imagine what it would be like to live in a place where it hardly ever rains, the sun bakes the soil, and very few plants grow. The world's deserts present a tough challenge to all living creatures, but amazingly, many different animals and plants have found ways to survive. The deserts are harsh but delicate places that are being threatened.

As the number of people in the world grows, we have turned to deserts to provide land for grazing animals, growing food, drilling for oil, and mining for precious metals.

All of this human activity is not only changing the way deserts look, it is also affecting the animals that make the desert their home. The delicate balance of nature, which brings life to the world's deserts, is in danger of being destroyed.

MAJOR DESERTS OF THE WORLD

Arctic Ocean

North Pacific Ocean

NORTH AMERICA

Great Salt Lake Desert

Black Rock Desert

Painted Desert

North Atlantic Ocean

Death Valley

Sonoran Desert

Mojave Desert

Chihuahuan Desert

Vizcaino Desert

South Pacific Ocean

SOUTH AMERICA

South Atlantic Ocean

Peruvian Desert

Atacama Desert

Patagonian Desert

Key

Named Desert areas

Unnamed Desert areas

Division between North and South America

Division between Asia and Africa

Division between Europe and Asia

Division between Asia and Oceania

4

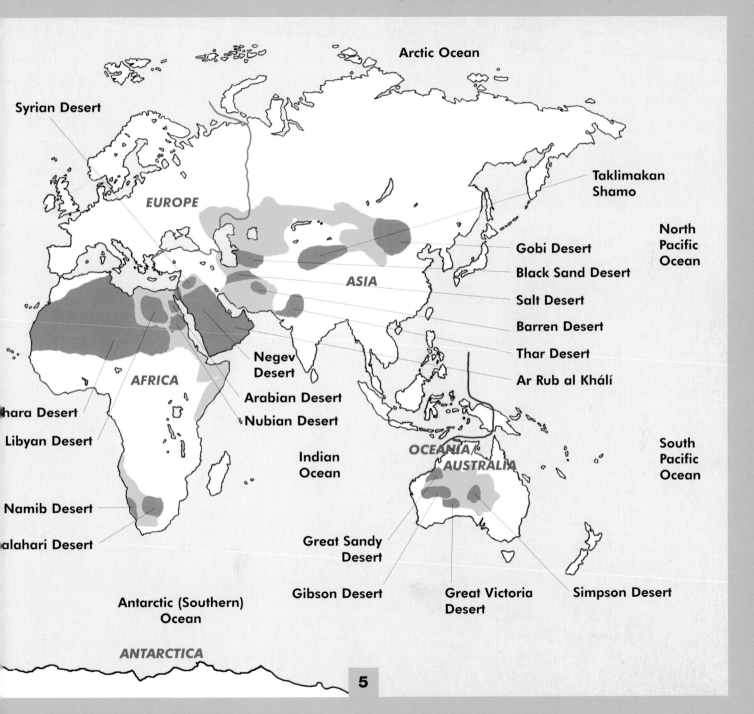

Arctic Ocean

Syrian Desert

EUROPE

Taklimakan
Shamo

North
Pacific
Ocean

Gobi Desert

Black Sand Desert

ASIA

Salt Desert

Barren Desert

Thar Desert

Negev
Desert

Ar Rub al Khálí

AFRICA

Arabian Desert

Nubian Desert

hara Desert

Libyan Desert

Indian
Ocean

OCEANIA

South
Pacific
Ocean

AUSTRALIA

Namib Desert

alahari Desert

Great Sandy
Desert

Antarctic (Southern)
Ocean

Gibson Desert

Great Victoria
Desert

Simpson Desert

ANTARCTICA

3 Deserts in the northern parts of Asia and North America are cold deserts. They have frozen ground and icy weather. The Gobi (left) in China and Mongolia is a cold desert.

1 A desert is one of the toughest places to live on Earth.

2 Most deserts have very hot days and cooler nights. The Sahara in Africa is a hot desert.

4 Deserts are dry. Rainfall each year is less than 10 inches (25 centimeters).

5 Deserts cover one-third of Earth's land surface, and they are located all over the world.

6 Deserts have been around for millions of years. They have formed in many different ways and at different times in history.

7 Some North American deserts may be as little as 10,000 years old. The land became drier, and parts of it received very little rain.

8 In the dry areas, plants withered and died. The wind blew away the soil, and the land became bare (right).

9 The slow drying of land created the Sahara and

Kalahari deserts of Africa and the Thar Desert of India and Pakistan.

10 Some deserts, such as the Mojave Desert in the United States (above), formed behind mountains. Most of the rain falls on the mountains, and little is left to fall on the other side.

11 The Australian deserts grew because they are in the middle of a large area of land. By the time air from the ocean reaches this area, it has little moisture.

12 The biggest desert on Earth is Africa's Sahara Desert. The Sahara covers about as much land as all of the United States.

13 **Temperatures** during the day in a hot desert may go up to 122° Fahrenheit (50° Celsius).

14 The hottest temperature ever recorded is 136.4° F (58° C), in El Azizia, Libya, which is in the Sahara area.

15 Desert skies have few clouds to block the sun, and shade trees cannot grow in the dry soil.

16 At night, however, the cloudless skies allow the heat of the day to escape quickly, and the temperature can drop below the **freezing point**.

17 The extreme range of temperatures and the shortage of water make it hard for animals, plants, or people to live in a desert.

18 The animals that live in deserts have **adaptations** to survive in the harsh conditions.

the insect tips over into a sort of headstand, and the water droplets trickle down its body and into its mouth.

21 Winged insects, such as locusts, can fly long distances in search of food and water.

19 In deserts near a seacoast, such as the Arabian Desert, insects can survive on water from fog and dew.

20 The darkling beetle (above) waits for dew to form on its back. Then,

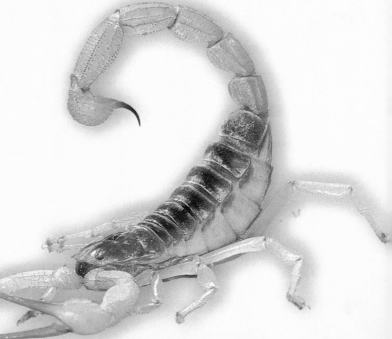

22 After a rainfall in the desert, some insects multiply quickly if food is plentiful. Locusts can form a **swarm** that covers up to 3,000 square miles (7,770 square kilometers).

23 The scorpion (left) stays safe in the desert by frightening its enemies with the poisonous stinger at the end of its tail.

24 For food, the scorpion captures lizards and smaller insects, crushing them to death in its claws.

25 The gila monster (above) and other **reptiles** can survive because they are cold-blooded. They use the air and land around their bodies to control their body temperature.

26 Because reptiles do not have to use their own energy to control their body temperature, they need less food, which is always in short supply in a desert.

27 Reptiles have scaly skin that helps keep moisture in their bodies and prevents them from drying out in the sun.

28 Lizards, such as the gecko (above), warm up in the morning sun. After their bodies are warm, they become more active. They can spend their time finding insects to eat.

29 Later in the day, the heat becomes more powerful, so lizards must find the cool shade under rocks and boulders.

30 Desert snakes, such as the Californian king snake (below) and the red spitting cobra from Africa, find shelter during the day and come out to hunt during the night.

31 Desert tortoises live in Mexico and the southern United States.

34 In the harsh desert weather, smaller mammals, such as **rodents**, find ways to scratch out a living.

32 When it is hottest, tortoises go to their burrows, or homes in the ground. They come out in the early morning and late afternoon to feed on plants.

35 Rodents that make their homes in the desert include gerbils, girds, jerboas, and mice. About forty **species** of rodents live in the Sahara Desert.

33 **Mammals** have the hardest time surviving in a desert. They are warm-blooded, which means they must control their own body temperature.

36 Gerbils (above) and some other rodents dig burrows under rocks. Taking shelter in burrows keeps these animals cooler in hot weather.

13

37 Small mammals go out in the evening to look for tufts of grass, fallen seeds, and bits of dead plants that the wind blows in. The animals survive on the tiny amount of moisture they get from plants.

38 Meerkats (left) live in groups in the African deserts. These mammals are insectivores, which means they eat insects.

39 Meerkats work in groups to find food. One meerkat serves as the lookout and gives a shrill cry when danger, such as an eagle or a jackal, is near.

40 The caracal, or desert lynx, (right) roams African and Asian deserts at night, hunting. These **predators** eat reptiles, birds, and mammals as large as **gazelles**.

41 In the wide-open desert, gazelles find safety by staying in herds of as many as fifty animals.

42 Desert predators get moisture from the blood of their prey.

43 Large ears are common among desert mammals, including the jack rabbit of North America, the fennec fox of the Sahara, and the desert hedgehog of the Gobi.

44 The animals' large ears help them hear all the sounds of the desert, especially the sounds that help them find food and stay away from predators.

46 The deserts of southern Africa provide a home for ground squirrels (right top), members of the rodent family.

47 Holding their bushy tails like small umbrellas, ground squirrels create their own shade to keep cool.

48 The scimitar-horned oryx (right bottom) is a herbivore, or plant eater. It grazes on grasses and other plants. These animals can go for long periods of

45 Large ears help fennec foxes (above) stay cool. Their ears have many tiny blood vessels that run very close to the surface of their skin. As air moves around their ears, it cools their blood, which helps cool their bodies.

were hunted so heavily by humans that very few of them are left in the wild.

50 Flying helps birds survive in the desert. They can search a large area for food and water.

time without having to search for water.

49 The scimitar-horned oryx and its close relative, the Arabian oryx,

51 The lanner falcon (right) is a Sahara Desert predator. It is a superb hunter.

52 Lanner falcons can catch birds in midair with their deadly **talons**, or they can swoop to the ground to pick up lizards.

53 Plants can protect birds that live in the desert. Some birds have trouble finding safe places to nest and lay eggs.

54 Ostriches (right), from North Africa, lay their eggs in the sand, a dangerous spot for chicks.

55 Ostrich chicks can run soon after they hatch, and their dull brown feathers help them hide.

56 To help them live in the desert, ostriches have powerful legs. They can run fast in the sand and kick animals that attack.

57 Although we often think of deserts as sandy, less than 20 percent of the desert area in the world is actually covered with sand.

58 Most deserts are covered with rocks, gravel, dust, or minerals, such as salt.

59 No matter what kind of material covers the desert, the wind shapes and changes it.

62 Sand dunes can be long, thin, and straight. They even form in the shape of huge stars.

63 Extreme hot and cold temperatures can cause rocks to crack, changing the shapes of rocky deserts.

60 The wind creates hills of sand called dunes. Some are as tall as 1,500 feet (455 meters).

61 The most common type of sand dune forms the curved shape of a crescent (above).

64 Wind blows dust and sand across a desert. The rough grains cut into cracks in the rock, widen them, and break them apart. Wind-blown sand can carve amazing formations into tall, rocky cliffs.

65 Some mountains in the desert have flat tops and steep cliffs. Others have rocky ledges that stick out like fingers.

66 The weather in the desert can stay the same for months or years.

67 Atacama Desert in northern Chile is the driest place on Earth. Parts of this desert have had no rain in over four hundred years.

68 In most deserts, long periods of dry weather are broken by thunderstorms (below) and heavy rain.

69 Desert storms, often fueled by powerful wind, can be violent.

70 The record amount of rainfall in the Sahara Desert is 1.75 inches (4.4 cm) in three hours.

71 In a desert storm, dry channels, called arroyos or **wadis**, can fill with rain very quickly. As the water races along, it can rip rock from the sides of a wadi or cause **flash floods**.

72 It is hard to believe, but more people have drowned in deserts during storms and floods than have died of thirst.

73 When enough rain falls, seeds that have lain **dormant** in dry soil for years can begin to sprout. After a heavy rain, a desert can spring to life.

74 Just days after rain falls, a desert that looked lifeless may become a colorful carpet of blooming flowers (left).

75 About 1,200 species of plants grow in the Sahara Desert. They have found many different ways of surviving in poor soil with little water.

76 Some desert plants, such as the creosote bush, grow wide, shallow networks of roots that can soak up rainwater as soon as it hits the ground.

77 Other plants, such as the tamarisk bush, have long webs of roots that dig down to reach moisture deep in the sand and rocks.

78 Cacti (left) are tough plants that can store water and use it in dry times. Their waxy stems help hold in the moisture.

79 The biggest cactus in the desert is the saguaro (below), which can grow up to 50 feet (15 m) tall. In one day, the saguaro can take in a ton of water.

80 Spadefoot toads of the southwestern United States lie low until a heavy rain falls. The toad uses a tough growth on each hind foot to bury itself 3 feet (1 m) under the ground, where it **hibernates.**

81 Even resting in their deep underground burrows, spadefoot toads can tell when rain is falling. They dig out and hop to the pools of rainwater (above).

82 The toads eat and breed in just a few days. Their young hatch, grow quickly, and then bury themselves to wait for the next heavy rain.

83 In some areas of a desert, water comes to Earth's surface from an underground spring or well. This water supports an area of plants called an **oasis** (right).

86 Some desert people live in permanent homes. Others are **nomads** who live in tents and move from place to place, usually with changes in the seasons or with their livestock.

84 Land in an oasis can be **fertile**, allowing crops to be grown.

85 In spite of the harsh conditions, some people do live in deserts.

87 The Tuareg is one of the largest groups of nomadic people who meet the challenges of desert life.

88 The Tuareg people travel through the Sahara on camels. Their loose-fitting clothes protect them from the heat.

89 Camels (above and right) are the true specialists of the desert. They have many **adaptations** to hot, sandy climates.

90 Camels have two toes connected by skin, and their feet spread out, making it easier for them to walk on sand.

91 If necessary, camels can eat thorny desert plants, twigs, and dry grass. When they don't have food, they can live off the fat stored in their humps.

92 Camels can go for days without water because their bodies lose

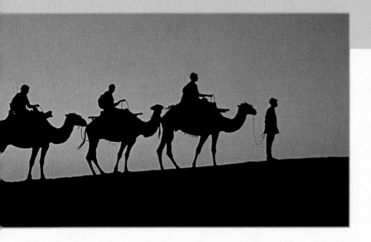

95 More land is turning into desert because the climate on Earth is slowly becoming warmer.

moisture slowly. They can drink 25 gallons (95 liters) of water in minutes.

96 People add to the growth of deserts by stripping the land of trees and causing **erosion**.

93 In the days before cars, camels were the main way to move things and people across a desert.

94 Over the last fifty years, deserts, such as the Sahara, have grown. This growth is not good news for Earth.

99 Machines that mine a desert's mineral deposits also hurt the environment.

97 If people try to grow too many crops on the edges of deserts, the soil becomes less fertile and then turns to dust.

98 To bring water to deserts, people have tried to pump it from nearby rivers or springs or from deep wells. In many cases, these projects have done more harm than good.

100 The way people use land today is spoiling once-fertile areas and upsetting the delicate balance of life in our deserts.

101 Deserts are home to unique and valuable plants and animals that survive scorching heat, icy cold, and desperately dry conditions. We must respect and protect Earth's deserts.

Glossary

adaptations: features that make survival easier in a certain place.

dormant: alive but not growing.

erosion: wearing away of the land by wind, water, or other forces.

fertile: full of nutrients plants need to grow.

flash floods: sudden floods in which the water level rises rapidly.

freezing point: the temperature at which water turns to ice.

gazelles: fast, graceful, deerlike animals with long horns

hibernates: goes into deep, long sleep until weather conditions become more suitable.

mammals: warm-blooded animals, such as cats, dogs, and humans, that have backbones and feed milk to their young.

nomads: desert people who do not live in a permanent home.

oasis: a place in the desert that gets water from an underground spring or well.

predators: animals that hunt other animals for food

reptiles: cold-blooded animals, such as lizards and snakes.

rodents: mammals that have teeth for gnawing.

species: types of animals or plants that are alike in many ways.

swarm: a gathering of insects.

talons: a hunting bird's claws.

temperature: a measurement of heat or cold.

wadis: dry river channels, also known as arroyos, that contain water only after rainfall.

More Books to Read

Crafts for Kids Who Are Wild About Deserts
Kathy Ross
(Millbrook Press)

Discovering Deserts
National Wildlife Federation
(McGraw Hill)

***In the Desert (Wild Wonders* series)**
Ann Cooper
(Roberts Rinehart)

***Living in a Desert (Welcome Books* series)**
Jan Kottke
(Children's Press)

Web Sites

Biomes of the World
mbgnet.mobot.org/sets/
desert/index.htm

Desert and Desert Animals
www.enchantedlearning.com/
biomes/desert/desert.shtml

Desert Resources
pubs.usgs.gov/gip/deserts/

Deserts
www.oxfam.org.uk/coolplanet/
ontheline/explore/nature/deserts/
deserts.htm

To find additional web sites, use a reliable search engine to find one or more of the following keywords: **desert, desert animals, Sahara**.

 # Index